50 Farmhouse Suppers Recipes

By: Kelly Johnson

Table of Contents

- Roast Chicken with Root Vegetables
- Beef and Barley Soup
- Buttermilk Biscuits with Sausage Gravy
- Baked Mac and Cheese with Breadcrumbs
- Chicken Pot Pie with Flaky Crust
- Meatloaf with Garlic Mashed Potatoes
- Biscuits and Gravy Casserole
- Cornbread and Chili
- Herb-Crusted Pork Roast with Apples
- Shepherd's Pie with Creamy Mashed Potatoes
- Southern Fried Chicken with Collard Greens
- Baked Ham with Maple Glaze
- Slow-Cooker Beef Stew
- Bacon-Wrapped Pork Tenderloin
- Chicken and Dumplings
- Roasted Brussels Sprouts with Bacon
- Country Fried Steak with Gravy

- Braised Short Ribs with Carrots and Potatoes
- Smothered Chicken with Rice
- Fried Green Tomatoes with Remoulade
- Sausage and Peppers Skillet
- Creamed Spinach and Garlic Bread
- Roast Duck with Cranberry Sauce
- Stuffed Bell Peppers with Ground Beef
- Slow-Cooked BBQ Ribs
- Pot Roast with Carrots and Onions
- Baked Ziti with Ground Sausage
- Chicken and Rice Casserole
- Braised Lamb Shanks with Mint
- Classic Beef Wellington
- Stuffed Chicken Breasts with Herbs and Cheese
- Squash Casserole with Cheese Topping
- Grilled Corn on the Cob with Herb Butter
- Baked Trout with Lemon and Dill
- Roasted Garlic Mashed Potatoes
- Corn Pudding with Jalapeños

- Chicken with Creamy Mushroom Sauce
- Sweet Potato Casserole with Marshmallows
- Grilled Pork Chops with Apple Chutney
- Roast Beef with Yorkshire Pudding
- Herb-Baked Salmon with Veggies
- Cabbage and Bacon Skillet
- Potatoes Au Gratin
- Creamy Potato Leek Soup
- Grilled Skirt Steak with Chimichurri
- Baked Chicken Thighs with Garlic and Thyme
- Quinoa Salad with Roasted Vegetables
- Roasted Beet and Goat Cheese Salad
- Classic Clam Chowder
- Chicken Fried Rice with Vegetables

Roast Chicken with Root Vegetables
 Ingredients:

- 1 whole chicken (3-4 lbs)
- 4 carrots, peeled and chopped
- 3 parsnips, peeled and chopped
- 1 sweet potato, peeled and chopped
- 2 tbsp olive oil
- 1 tbsp fresh thyme
- 1 tbsp fresh rosemary
- 4 garlic cloves, smashed
- Salt and pepper

Instructions:

1. Preheat the oven to 400°F (200°C).
2. Rub the chicken with olive oil, thyme, rosemary, garlic, salt, and pepper.
3. Toss the chopped root vegetables with olive oil, salt, and pepper, and spread them on a roasting pan.
4. Place the chicken on top of the vegetables and roast for 1 hour and 20 minutes, or until the chicken reaches 165°F (74°C) and the vegetables are tender.
5. Let rest before carving and serving.

Beef and Barley Soup
  Ingredients:

- 1 lb stew beef, cubed
- 1 onion, chopped
- 2 carrots, chopped
- 2 celery stalks, chopped
- 1/2 cup barley
- 4 cups beef broth
- 1 tsp thyme
- 1 bay leaf
- Salt and pepper

Instructions:

1. Brown the stew beef in a large pot with some oil.
2. Add the onions, carrots, and celery and sauté for 5 minutes.
3. Stir in the barley, beef broth, thyme, bay leaf, salt, and pepper.
4. Bring to a boil, then reduce the heat and simmer for 1-1.5 hours until the beef is tender and the barley is cooked.
5. Remove the bay leaf and serve hot.

Buttermilk Biscuits with Sausage Gravy

Ingredients:

For Biscuits:

- 2 cups all-purpose flour
- 1 tbsp baking powder
- 1/2 tsp salt
- 1/2 cup cold butter, cubed
- 3/4 cup buttermilk

For Sausage Gravy:

- 1 lb breakfast sausage
- 1/4 cup all-purpose flour
- 2 cups milk
- Salt and pepper

Instructions:

1. Preheat oven to 450°F (230°C).
2. For the biscuits, combine flour, baking powder, and salt in a bowl. Cut in butter until crumbly. Stir in buttermilk to form a dough.
3. Pat the dough onto a floured surface, fold it over several times, and cut into rounds.
4. Bake for 10-12 minutes, until golden brown.

5. For the gravy, cook sausage in a pan until browned, then sprinkle with flour and stir for 1 minute.

6. Gradually add milk, stirring until thickened. Season with salt and pepper.

7. Serve the biscuits with sausage gravy on top.

Baked Mac and Cheese with Breadcrumbs

Ingredients:

- 8 oz elbow macaroni
- 2 tbsp butter
- 2 tbsp flour
- 2 cups milk
- 2 cups shredded cheddar cheese
- 1/2 cup grated Parmesan
- 1 cup breadcrumbs
- Salt and pepper

Instructions:

1. Preheat oven to 350°F (175°C).
2. Cook macaroni according to package instructions, then drain.
3. In a saucepan, melt butter and whisk in flour to make a roux. Slowly add milk, stirring until thickened.
4. Stir in cheddar cheese and Parmesan until melted. Season with salt and pepper.
5. Mix the sauce with the cooked macaroni and transfer to a baking dish. Top with breadcrumbs.
6. Bake for 20 minutes until bubbly and golden brown on top.

Chicken Pot Pie with Flaky Crust
Ingredients:

- 2 cups cooked chicken, shredded
- 2 cups mixed vegetables (peas, carrots, corn)
- 1/3 cup butter
- 1/3 cup flour
- 2 cups chicken broth
- 1 cup milk
- 1 tsp thyme
- Salt and pepper
- 1 sheet puff pastry or pie crust

Instructions:

1. Preheat oven to 400°F (200°C).
2. In a pan, melt butter and whisk in flour to make a roux. Gradually add chicken broth and milk, stirring until thickened.
3. Stir in chicken, vegetables, thyme, salt, and pepper.
4. Roll out the puff pastry and fit it over a baking dish. Fill with the chicken mixture.
5. Bake for 25-30 minutes, until golden and flaky.

Meatloaf with Garlic Mashed Potatoes

Ingredients:

For Meatloaf:

- 1 lb ground beef
- 1/2 cup breadcrumbs
- 1/4 cup milk
- 1 egg
- 1/4 cup onion, chopped
- 2 tbsp ketchup
- 1 tbsp Worcestershire sauce
- Salt and pepper

For Mashed Potatoes:

- 4 large potatoes, peeled and chopped
- 1/2 cup butter
- 1/2 cup milk
- 2 garlic cloves, minced
- Salt and pepper

Instructions:

1. Preheat oven to 375°F (190°C).

2. For the meatloaf, mix all ingredients in a bowl. Form into a loaf and place on a baking sheet.

3. Bake for 45 minutes.

4. For the mashed potatoes, boil potatoes until tender, then drain.

5. Mash with butter, milk, garlic, salt, and pepper.

6. Serve meatloaf with mashed potatoes.

Biscuits and Gravy Casserole

Ingredients:

- 1 can biscuit dough
- 1 lb breakfast sausage
- 2 cups milk
- 1/4 cup flour
- Salt and pepper

Instructions:

1. Preheat oven to 350°F (175°C).
2. Brown sausage in a pan, then sprinkle with flour and stir for 1 minute.
3. Add milk and stir until thickened.
4. Cut biscuit dough into pieces and place in a casserole dish.
5. Pour sausage gravy over the biscuits and bake for 20-25 minutes.

Cornbread and Chili

Ingredients:

For Cornbread:

- 1 cup cornmeal
- 1 cup flour
- 1/4 cup sugar
- 1 tbsp baking powder
- 1 cup milk
- 1/4 cup melted butter
- 2 eggs

For Chili:

- 1 lb ground beef
- 1 onion, chopped
- 1 can kidney beans
- 1 can diced tomatoes
- 1 tbsp chili powder
- Salt and pepper

Instructions:

1. Preheat oven to 400°F (200°C).

2. For the cornbread, mix dry ingredients and wet ingredients separately, then combine.

3. Pour into a greased pan and bake for 20-25 minutes.

4. For the chili, brown ground beef with onion, then add beans, tomatoes, chili powder, salt, and pepper. Simmer for 20 minutes.

5. Serve chili with cornbread.

Herb-Crusted Pork Roast with Apples

Ingredients:

- 1 pork roast (3-4 lbs)
- 2 apples, sliced
- 2 tbsp olive oil
- 1 tbsp rosemary
- 1 tbsp thyme
- Salt and pepper

Instructions:

1. Preheat oven to 375°F (190°C).
2. Rub the pork roast with olive oil, rosemary, thyme, salt, and pepper.
3. Place in a roasting pan with apple slices and roast for 1-1.5 hours, until internal temperature reaches 145°F (63°C).
4. Let rest before slicing.

Shepherd's Pie with Creamy Mashed Potatoes

Ingredients:

- 1 lb ground lamb or beef
- 1 onion, chopped
- 2 carrots, chopped
- 1 cup peas
- 2 cups mashed potatoes
- 1 tbsp Worcestershire sauce
- 1/2 cup beef broth
- Salt and pepper

Instructions:

1. Preheat oven to 400°F (200°C).
2. Brown the ground meat with onion and carrots. Add peas, Worcestershire sauce, beef broth, salt, and pepper.
3. Pour into a baking dish and top with mashed potatoes.
4. Bake for 20-25 minutes, until the top is golden.

Southern Fried Chicken with Collard Greens

Ingredients:

For Chicken:

- 4 chicken pieces
- 1 cup buttermilk
- 1 cup flour
- 1 tsp paprika
- 1 tsp garlic powder
- Salt and pepper

For Collard Greens:

- 1 lb collard greens, chopped
- 1 tbsp olive oil
- 1 onion, chopped
- 1 garlic clove, minced
- 1 cup chicken broth

Instructions:

1. For the chicken, soak in buttermilk for at least 30 minutes.
2. Coat in seasoned flour and fry in hot oil until crispy.
3. For collard greens, sauté onion and garlic, then add greens and chicken broth. Simmer for 20-25 minutes.

4. Serve fried chicken with collard greens.

Baked Ham with Maple Glaze

Ingredients:

- 1 whole ham (5-6 lbs)
- 1/2 cup maple syrup
- 1/4 cup Dijon mustard
- 1/4 cup brown sugar
- 1/4 cup apple cider vinegar
- 1 tsp ground cinnamon
- Salt and pepper

Instructions:

1. Preheat the oven to 325°F (165°C).
2. Score the ham with shallow cuts in a diamond pattern.
3. Mix the maple syrup, mustard, brown sugar, apple cider vinegar, cinnamon, salt, and pepper in a bowl.
4. Brush the ham with the glaze, then place it in the oven.
5. Roast for 1.5-2 hours, basting every 30 minutes with more glaze.
6. Let rest before carving.

Slow-Cooker Beef Stew

Ingredients:

- 2 lbs beef stew meat, cubed
- 4 carrots, chopped
- 3 potatoes, cubed
- 1 onion, chopped
- 3 cloves garlic, minced
- 4 cups beef broth
- 1 cup red wine (optional)
- 2 tbsp tomato paste
- 2 tsp thyme
- Salt and pepper

Instructions:

1. Add the beef, carrots, potatoes, onion, and garlic to the slow cooker.
2. In a bowl, whisk together beef broth, red wine (if using), tomato paste, thyme, salt, and pepper.
3. Pour over the meat and vegetables.
4. Cover and cook on low for 7-8 hours or until the beef is tender.
5. Serve hot with crusty bread.

Bacon-Wrapped Pork Tenderloin

Ingredients:

- 1 pork tenderloin (1.5-2 lbs)
- 10 slices of bacon
- 2 tbsp olive oil
- 1 tbsp rosemary
- 1 tsp garlic powder
- Salt and pepper

Instructions:

1. Preheat the oven to 375°F (190°C).
2. Season the pork tenderloin with rosemary, garlic powder, salt, and pepper.
3. Wrap the pork with the bacon slices, securing with toothpicks.
4. Heat olive oil in a skillet and sear the bacon-wrapped pork on all sides until golden brown.
5. Transfer to the oven and roast for 25-30 minutes, or until the pork reaches 145°F (63°C).
6. Let rest before slicing.

Chicken and Dumplings
 Ingredients:

- 4 boneless, skinless chicken breasts
- 4 cups chicken broth
- 1 cup heavy cream
- 1 onion, chopped
- 3 carrots, chopped
- 2 celery stalks, chopped
- 1 tsp thyme
- Salt and pepper
- 1 cup all-purpose flour
- 2 tsp baking powder
- 1/4 cup butter
- 1/4 cup milk

Instructions:

1. In a large pot, cook the chicken breasts in chicken broth until fully cooked. Remove the chicken, shred it, and set it aside.
2. In the same pot, sauté onion, carrots, and celery until soft.
3. Add the shredded chicken, cream, thyme, salt, and pepper to the pot.
4. In a separate bowl, mix flour, baking powder, butter, and milk to form a dough.

5. Drop spoonfuls of the dough into the soup and cover. Let simmer for 20 minutes, until the dumplings are cooked through.

6. Serve hot with a sprinkle of parsley.

Roasted Brussels Sprouts with Bacon

Ingredients:

- 1 lb Brussels sprouts, halved
- 6 slices bacon, chopped
- 2 tbsp olive oil
- 1 tbsp balsamic vinegar
- Salt and pepper

Instructions:

1. Preheat oven to 400°F (200°C).
2. In a pan, cook the bacon until crispy, then drain on paper towels.
3. Toss Brussels sprouts with olive oil, salt, and pepper, and spread on a baking sheet.
4. Roast for 20-25 minutes, shaking the pan halfway through.
5. Drizzle with balsamic vinegar and sprinkle with crispy bacon before serving.

Country Fried Steak with Gravy
Ingredients:

- 4 beef cube steaks
- 1 cup flour
- 1 tsp garlic powder
- 1 tsp onion powder
- 1 tsp paprika
- Salt and pepper
- 1 cup buttermilk
- 1/4 cup oil for frying

For Gravy:

- 2 tbsp flour
- 2 cups milk
- Salt and pepper

Instructions:

1. Season the cube steaks with salt and pepper.
2. Dredge in a mixture of flour, garlic powder, onion powder, paprika, salt, and pepper.
3. Dip in buttermilk, then back in the flour mixture.

4. Heat oil in a pan and fry steaks until golden brown and crispy, about 4-5 minutes per side.

5. For the gravy, in the same pan, whisk in flour and cook for 1 minute. Gradually add milk, stirring until thickened.

6. Serve the steaks with the gravy on top.

Braised Short Ribs with Carrots and Potatoes
Ingredients:

- 4 beef short ribs
- 2 tbsp olive oil
- 2 carrots, chopped
- 2 potatoes, cubed
- 1 onion, chopped
- 3 garlic cloves, minced
- 2 cups red wine
- 2 cups beef broth
- 1 tbsp thyme
- Salt and pepper

Instructions:

1. Preheat oven to 350°F (175°C).
2. Brown short ribs in olive oil in a large pot.
3. Remove ribs and sauté onion, garlic, carrots, and potatoes in the same pot.
4. Add wine, beef broth, thyme, salt, and pepper. Return short ribs to the pot.
5. Cover and braise in the oven for 2.5-3 hours, until tender.
6. Serve hot with vegetables.

Smothered Chicken with Rice
Ingredients:

- 4 chicken breasts
- 1 onion, chopped
- 1 bell pepper, chopped
- 2 garlic cloves, minced
- 1 can cream of mushroom soup
- 1 cup chicken broth
- 1 tsp thyme
- Salt and pepper
- 2 cups cooked rice

Instructions:

1. Season chicken breasts with salt and pepper. Brown on both sides in a skillet, then remove.
2. Sauté onion, bell pepper, and garlic in the same skillet.
3. Add mushroom soup, chicken broth, thyme, salt, and pepper. Stir until combined.
4. Return chicken breasts to the pan and simmer for 20-25 minutes, until cooked through.
5. Serve the smothered chicken over rice.

Fried Green Tomatoes with Remoulade
Ingredients:

- 4 green tomatoes, sliced
- 1 cup buttermilk
- 1 cup cornmeal
- 1/2 cup flour
- 1 tsp paprika
- Salt and pepper
- Oil for frying

For Remoulade:

- 1/2 cup mayonnaise
- 1 tbsp Dijon mustard
- 1 tbsp horseradish
- 1 tbsp lemon juice
- 1/2 tsp paprika
- Salt and pepper

Instructions:

1. Heat oil in a frying pan.
2. Dip tomato slices in buttermilk, then dredge in cornmeal, flour, paprika, salt, and pepper.

3. Fry tomatoes in batches until golden brown, about 2-3 minutes per side.

4. For the remoulade, mix all ingredients in a bowl.

5. Serve fried green tomatoes with remoulade sauce.

Sausage and Peppers Skillet

Ingredients:

- 4 sausage links (Italian or your choice)
- 2 bell peppers, sliced
- 1 onion, sliced
- 2 garlic cloves, minced
- 1 tbsp olive oil
- Salt and pepper

Instructions:

1. Brown the sausage links in a skillet, then remove and slice.
2. In the same skillet, sauté peppers, onion, and garlic in olive oil until softened.
3. Return sausage slices to the pan and cook for another 5 minutes.
4. Serve hot with a side of crusty bread.

Creamed Spinach and Garlic Bread
Ingredients:

- 4 cups fresh spinach, chopped
- 1/2 cup heavy cream
- 2 tbsp butter
- 2 garlic cloves, minced
- Salt and pepper
- 1 loaf French bread
- 1/4 cup butter, melted
- 2 cloves garlic, minced

Instructions:

1. For the creamed spinach, sauté garlic in butter until fragrant, then add spinach and cook until wilted.
2. Add cream, salt, and pepper and simmer until thickened.
3. For garlic bread, brush French bread with melted butter, sprinkle with garlic, and toast in the oven at 375°F (190°C) for 10-12 minutes.
4. Serve creamed spinach alongside garlic bread.

Roast Duck with Cranberry Sauce

Ingredients:

- 1 whole duck (4-5 lbs)
- 2 tbsp olive oil
- 1 tsp thyme
- 1 tsp rosemary
- Salt and pepper
- 1 cup cranberry sauce

Instructions:

1. Preheat oven to 350°F (175°C).
2. Pat the duck dry and rub with olive oil, thyme, rosemary, salt, and pepper.
3. Roast the duck in a roasting pan for 1.5-2 hours, until the skin is crispy and golden.
4. Heat cranberry sauce in a saucepan over low heat.
5. Serve the duck with the warm cranberry sauce on top.

Stuffed Bell Peppers with Ground Beef

Ingredients:

- 4 large bell peppers
- 1 lb ground beef
- 1 onion, chopped
- 2 cloves garlic, minced
- 1 can diced tomatoes
- 1 cup cooked rice
- 1 tsp oregano
- 1 tsp basil
- Salt and pepper
- 1 cup shredded cheese (optional)

Instructions:

1. Preheat oven to 375°F (190°C).
2. Cut the tops off the peppers and remove seeds.
3. In a skillet, cook the ground beef with onion and garlic until browned.
4. Add the diced tomatoes, rice, oregano, basil, salt, and pepper. Stir to combine.
5. Stuff the peppers with the beef mixture and place in a baking dish.
6. Cover with foil and bake for 25-30 minutes.

7. Top with cheese and bake uncovered for an additional 5 minutes until cheese is melted.

Slow-Cooked BBQ Ribs

Ingredients:

- 2 racks of baby back ribs
- 1 cup BBQ sauce
- 1 tsp paprika
- 1 tsp garlic powder
- 1 tsp onion powder
- Salt and pepper

Instructions:

1. Preheat the slow cooker to low heat.
2. Rub the ribs with paprika, garlic powder, onion powder, salt, and pepper.
3. Place ribs in the slow cooker and pour BBQ sauce over the top.
4. Cook for 6-8 hours, until the ribs are tender and the meat pulls away from the bone.
5. Serve with extra BBQ sauce.

Pot Roast with Carrots and Onions

Ingredients:

- 3-4 lb beef chuck roast
- 1 onion, chopped
- 4 carrots, chopped
- 2 cups beef broth
- 2 tbsp olive oil
- 2 cloves garlic, minced
- 1 tsp thyme
- 1 tsp rosemary
- Salt and pepper

Instructions:

1. Preheat oven to 350°F (175°C).
2. Season the roast with salt and pepper.
3. Heat olive oil in a large Dutch oven and brown the roast on all sides.
4. Remove the roast and sauté the onion, garlic, and carrots in the same pot.
5. Return the roast to the pot and add beef broth, thyme, and rosemary.
6. Cover and roast for 3-4 hours, until tender.
7. Slice and serve with the vegetables.

Baked Ziti with Ground Sausage

Ingredients:

- 1 lb ziti pasta
- 1 lb ground sausage
- 2 cups marinara sauce
- 2 cups shredded mozzarella cheese
- 1/2 cup grated Parmesan cheese
- 1/4 cup chopped fresh basil

Instructions:

1. Preheat oven to 375°F (190°C).
2. Cook ziti pasta according to package directions, then drain.
3. In a skillet, cook the ground sausage until browned.
4. Add marinara sauce to the sausage and stir.
5. Combine cooked ziti, sausage mixture, and 1 cup of mozzarella cheese in a baking dish.
6. Top with the remaining mozzarella and Parmesan cheeses.
7. Bake for 25-30 minutes, until cheese is melted and bubbly.
8. Garnish with fresh basil before serving.

Chicken and Rice Casserole

Ingredients:

- 2 cups cooked chicken, shredded
- 2 cups cooked rice
- 1 can cream of chicken soup
- 1/2 cup sour cream
- 1 cup shredded cheddar cheese
- 1 cup chicken broth
- 1 tsp garlic powder
- 1 tsp onion powder
- Salt and pepper

Instructions:

1. Preheat oven to 350°F (175°C).
2. In a bowl, combine cooked chicken, rice, cream of chicken soup, sour cream, chicken broth, garlic powder, onion powder, salt, and pepper.
3. Pour into a greased casserole dish and top with shredded cheddar cheese.
4. Bake for 25-30 minutes until bubbly and golden on top.
5. Serve hot.

Braised Lamb Shanks with Mint

Ingredients:

- 4 lamb shanks
- 2 tbsp olive oil
- 1 onion, chopped
- 2 cloves garlic, minced
- 1 cup red wine
- 2 cups beef broth
- 1 tsp rosemary
- 1 tsp thyme
- Salt and pepper
- Fresh mint for garnish

Instructions:

1. Preheat oven to 325°F (165°C).
2. Season lamb shanks with salt and pepper.
3. Heat olive oil in a large Dutch oven and brown the lamb shanks on all sides.
4. Remove shanks and sauté onion and garlic in the same pot.
5. Add wine, beef broth, rosemary, and thyme. Stir to combine.
6. Return lamb shanks to the pot and cover.
7. Braise in the oven for 2.5-3 hours, until the meat is tender and falls off the bone.

8. Garnish with fresh mint and serve.

Classic Beef Wellington

Ingredients:

- 1.5 lb beef tenderloin
- 1/4 cup Dijon mustard
- 8 oz mushrooms, finely chopped
- 2 tbsp butter
- 1/4 cup pâté (optional)
- 1 sheet puff pastry
- 1 egg, beaten
- Salt and pepper

Instructions:

1. Preheat oven to 400°F (200°C).
2. Sear the beef tenderloin in a hot pan for 2-3 minutes on each side, then brush with Dijon mustard.
3. Sauté mushrooms in butter until dry, then let cool.
4. Roll out the puff pastry and layer with pâté (optional) and the sautéed mushrooms.
5. Place the beef in the center, then wrap it in the pastry.
6. Brush with egg wash and bake for 25-30 minutes, until golden brown.
7. Let rest for 10 minutes before slicing and serving.

Stuffed Chicken Breasts with Herbs and Cheese
Ingredients:

- 4 boneless, skinless chicken breasts
- 1 cup spinach, chopped
- 1/2 cup cream cheese
- 1/2 cup shredded mozzarella cheese
- 1 tbsp garlic powder
- 1 tbsp onion powder
- 1 tsp thyme
- Salt and pepper

Instructions:

1. Preheat oven to 375°F (190°C).
2. Mix spinach, cream cheese, mozzarella cheese, garlic powder, onion powder, thyme, salt, and pepper in a bowl.
3. Cut a pocket into each chicken breast and stuff with the cheese mixture.
4. Season the outside of the chicken with salt and pepper.
5. Bake for 25-30 minutes, until the chicken is cooked through and the filling is melted.
6. Serve hot.

Squash Casserole with Cheese Topping

Ingredients:

- 4 cups yellow squash, sliced
- 1 onion, chopped
- 1 cup shredded cheddar cheese
- 1/2 cup breadcrumbs
- 1/2 cup sour cream
- 2 eggs, beaten
- 1 tsp thyme
- Salt and pepper

Instructions:

1. Preheat oven to 350°F (175°C).
2. Sauté squash and onion in a pan until soft.
3. In a bowl, combine squash mixture, cheese, breadcrumbs, sour cream, eggs, thyme, salt, and pepper.
4. Transfer to a greased baking dish and top with more breadcrumbs.
5. Bake for 25-30 minutes, until the top is golden and bubbly.

Grilled Corn on the Cob with Herb Butter

Ingredients:

- 4 ears of corn, husked
- 1/2 cup butter, softened
- 2 tbsp chopped fresh herbs (parsley, thyme, or cilantro)
- Salt and pepper

Instructions:

1. Preheat grill to medium-high heat.
2. Grill corn for 10-15 minutes, turning occasionally, until charred.
3. Mix butter with herbs, salt, and pepper.
4. Brush the grilled corn with herb butter and serve immediately.

Baked Trout with Lemon and Dill

Ingredients:

- 4 trout fillets
- 2 tbsp olive oil
- 1 lemon, sliced
- 2 tbsp fresh dill, chopped
- Salt and pepper

Instructions:

1. Preheat oven to 375°F (190°C).
2. Place trout fillets on a baking sheet lined with parchment paper.
3. Drizzle with olive oil and season with salt and pepper.
4. Top with lemon slices and sprinkle with fresh dill.
5. Bake for 12-15 minutes, until the fish flakes easily with a fork.
6. Serve with additional lemon wedges.

Roasted Garlic Mashed Potatoes

Ingredients:

- 2 lbs russet potatoes, peeled and cubed
- 1 head garlic, roasted
- 4 tbsp butter
- 1/2 cup heavy cream
- Salt and pepper

Instructions:

1. Boil potatoes in salted water for 15-20 minutes, until tender.
2. While potatoes cook, roast garlic: cut the top off the garlic head, drizzle with olive oil, wrap in foil, and bake at 400°F (200°C) for 30 minutes.
3. Once garlic is cool enough to handle, squeeze the cloves into a bowl.
4. Drain potatoes and return them to the pot.
5. Mash with butter, heavy cream, roasted garlic, salt, and pepper until smooth and creamy.
6. Serve hot.

Corn Pudding with Jalapeños
Ingredients:

- 1 can (15 oz) corn kernels, drained
- 1 cup milk
- 1/2 cup heavy cream
- 3 large eggs
- 1/2 cup cornmeal
- 1/4 cup flour
- 2 jalapeños, finely chopped
- 1 cup shredded cheddar cheese
- 1 tbsp butter, melted
- Salt and pepper

Instructions:

1. Preheat oven to 350°F (175°C).
2. Whisk together milk, heavy cream, eggs, melted butter, and cornmeal in a bowl.
3. Stir in corn kernels, jalapeños, cheese, flour, salt, and pepper.
4. Pour the mixture into a greased baking dish.
5. Bake for 45-50 minutes, until the center is set and the top is golden.
6. Let cool for a few minutes before serving.

Chicken with Creamy Mushroom Sauce

Ingredients:

- 4 boneless, skinless chicken breasts
- 2 tbsp olive oil
- 1 onion, chopped
- 2 cups mushrooms, sliced
- 1 cup heavy cream
- 1/2 cup chicken broth
- 1 tbsp Dijon mustard
- 2 cloves garlic, minced
- Salt and pepper

Instructions:

1. Season chicken breasts with salt and pepper.
2. Heat olive oil in a large skillet over medium heat.
3. Cook chicken for 5-6 minutes per side, until golden brown and cooked through.
4. Remove chicken and set aside.
5. In the same skillet, sauté onions, garlic, and mushrooms until soft.
6. Add chicken broth, mustard, and heavy cream. Stir to combine and simmer for 5 minutes.
7. Return chicken to the skillet and simmer in the sauce for an additional 5 minutes.

8. Serve the chicken with the creamy mushroom sauce.

Sweet Potato Casserole with Marshmallows
Ingredients:

- 4 large sweet potatoes, peeled and cubed
- 1/2 cup brown sugar
- 1/4 cup butter, melted
- 1 tsp cinnamon
- 1/2 tsp nutmeg
- 1/2 cup heavy cream
- 1 cup mini marshmallows

Instructions:

1. Preheat oven to 350°F (175°C).
2. Boil sweet potatoes for 10-15 minutes until tender. Drain and mash.
3. Mix mashed sweet potatoes with brown sugar, melted butter, cinnamon, nutmeg, and heavy cream.
4. Transfer the mixture to a greased baking dish.
5. Top with mini marshmallows.
6. Bake for 20-25 minutes, until the marshmallows are golden and melted.

Grilled Pork Chops with Apple Chutney

Ingredients:

- 4 pork chops
- 2 tbsp olive oil
- 1 tbsp rosemary, chopped
- Salt and pepper
- 2 apples, peeled and chopped
- 1/4 cup onion, chopped
- 1/4 cup brown sugar
- 1/4 cup apple cider vinegar
- 1/4 tsp cinnamon

Instructions:

1. Preheat the grill to medium-high heat.
2. Rub pork chops with olive oil, rosemary, salt, and pepper.
3. Grill the pork chops for 6-7 minutes per side, until the internal temperature reaches 145°F (63°C).
4. While grilling, cook apples and onions in a saucepan with brown sugar, apple cider vinegar, and cinnamon. Simmer for 10-15 minutes until the chutney thickens.
5. Serve pork chops with apple chutney on top.

Roast Beef with Yorkshire Pudding

Ingredients:

- 3 lb beef roast
- 2 tbsp olive oil
- 2 tsp rosemary
- Salt and pepper
- 1 cup flour
- 1/2 cup milk
- 2 eggs
- 1/2 tsp salt

Instructions:

1. Preheat oven to 375°F (190°C).
2. Rub beef roast with olive oil, rosemary, salt, and pepper.
3. Roast beef for 1.5-2 hours, until the internal temperature reaches 135°F (57°C) for medium-rare.
4. While the beef cooks, make the Yorkshire pudding batter: whisk together flour, milk, eggs, and salt.
5. Pour the batter into a hot, greased muffin tin and bake for 15-20 minutes until puffed and golden.
6. Slice the roast beef and serve with Yorkshire pudding.

Herb-Baked Salmon with Veggies
Ingredients:

- 4 salmon fillets
- 1 lemon, sliced
- 2 tbsp olive oil
- 1 tbsp thyme, chopped
- 1 tbsp rosemary, chopped
- 1 cup broccoli florets
- 1 cup baby carrots
- Salt and pepper

Instructions:

1. Preheat oven to 400°F (200°C).
2. Place salmon fillets on a baking sheet and drizzle with olive oil.
3. Sprinkle with thyme, rosemary, salt, and pepper. Top with lemon slices.
4. Add broccoli and carrots around the salmon.
5. Bake for 12-15 minutes, until the salmon flakes easily with a fork.
6. Serve immediately.

Cabbage and Bacon Skillet

Ingredients:

- 1/2 head of cabbage, chopped
- 6 slices bacon, chopped
- 1 onion, chopped
- 2 cloves garlic, minced
- 1/2 tsp smoked paprika
- Salt and pepper

Instructions:

1. Cook bacon in a skillet over medium heat until crispy.
2. Remove bacon and set aside, leaving some fat in the skillet.
3. Sauté onion and garlic in the bacon fat until softened.
4. Add cabbage and smoked paprika, cooking for 8-10 minutes until tender.
5. Stir in the cooked bacon, and season with salt and pepper.
6. Serve hot.

Potatoes Au Gratin

Ingredients:

- 4 large russet potatoes, thinly sliced
- 2 cups heavy cream
- 1 cup whole milk
- 2 cups shredded Gruyère cheese
- 1 cup grated Parmesan cheese
- 2 cloves garlic, minced
- 2 tbsp butter, melted
- 1 tbsp fresh thyme, chopped
- Salt and pepper

Instructions:

1. Preheat oven to 375°F (190°C).
2. Grease a baking dish with butter.
3. In a saucepan, heat the cream, milk, garlic, salt, and pepper over medium heat until warm.
4. Layer the sliced potatoes in the baking dish, slightly overlapping each slice.
5. Pour the warm cream mixture over the potatoes. Sprinkle with Gruyère, Parmesan, and thyme.
6. Cover with foil and bake for 45 minutes.

7. Remove the foil and bake for an additional 15 minutes, until the top is golden brown and the potatoes are tender.

8. Let cool for a few minutes before serving.

Creamy Potato Leek Soup

Ingredients:

- 4 large potatoes, peeled and cubed
- 2 leeks, cleaned and sliced
- 1 medium onion, chopped
- 2 cloves garlic, minced
- 4 cups vegetable or chicken broth
- 1 cup heavy cream
- 2 tbsp butter
- Salt and pepper
- Fresh chives, chopped (for garnish)

Instructions:

1. In a large pot, melt butter over medium heat.
2. Add leeks, onions, and garlic. Sauté for 5-7 minutes, until softened.
3. Add potatoes, broth, salt, and pepper. Bring to a boil, then reduce heat and simmer for 20-25 minutes, until the potatoes are tender.
4. Use an immersion blender to blend the soup until smooth and creamy.
5. Stir in the heavy cream and adjust seasoning as needed.
6. Serve hot, garnished with chopped chives.

Grilled Skirt Steak with Chimichurri

Ingredients:

- 1 lb skirt steak
- 2 tbsp olive oil
- Salt and pepper
- 1 cup fresh parsley
- 3 cloves garlic
- 2 tbsp red wine vinegar
- 1 tsp red pepper flakes
- 1/2 cup olive oil
- 1 tbsp oregano

Instructions:

1. Preheat the grill to medium-high heat.
2. Season the skirt steak with olive oil, salt, and pepper. Grill for 4-5 minutes per side for medium-rare, or longer for your preferred doneness.
3. In a food processor, combine parsley, garlic, red wine vinegar, red pepper flakes, olive oil, oregano, salt, and pepper. Blend until smooth.
4. Let the steak rest for a few minutes before slicing.
5. Serve the steak slices with chimichurri sauce on top.

Baked Chicken Thighs with Garlic and Thyme

Ingredients:

- 4 bone-in, skin-on chicken thighs
- 4 cloves garlic, minced
- 2 tbsp fresh thyme, chopped
- 2 tbsp olive oil
- Salt and pepper
- 1 lemon, sliced

Instructions:

1. Preheat oven to 400°F (200°C).
2. In a small bowl, mix garlic, thyme, olive oil, salt, and pepper.
3. Rub the chicken thighs with the garlic mixture, making sure they are well coated.
4. Arrange the chicken thighs on a baking sheet and place lemon slices around them.
5. Bake for 35-40 minutes, until the chicken reaches an internal temperature of 165°F (74°C) and the skin is crispy.
6. Serve hot with the roasted lemon slices.

Quinoa Salad with Roasted Vegetables
Ingredients:

- 1 cup quinoa, rinsed
- 2 cups vegetable broth
- 1 zucchini, diced
- 1 red bell pepper, diced
- 1/2 red onion, diced
- 1 tbsp olive oil
- 1 tsp cumin
- Salt and pepper
- 1/4 cup feta cheese, crumbled
- 2 tbsp fresh parsley, chopped
- 1 tbsp lemon juice

Instructions:

1. Preheat oven to 400°F (200°C).
2. Toss the zucchini, bell pepper, and onion with olive oil, cumin, salt, and pepper. Spread the vegetables on a baking sheet and roast for 20-25 minutes, until tender.
3. Meanwhile, cook quinoa: bring vegetable broth to a boil in a medium saucepan. Add quinoa, reduce heat, and simmer for 15 minutes, until the liquid is absorbed and the quinoa is tender.

4. In a large bowl, combine quinoa, roasted vegetables, feta, parsley, and lemon juice. Toss to combine.

5. Serve at room temperature or chilled.

Roasted Beet and Goat Cheese Salad

Ingredients:

- 4 medium beets, peeled and cubed
- 2 tbsp olive oil
- Salt and pepper
- 4 cups mixed greens
- 1/4 cup goat cheese, crumbled
- 1/4 cup walnuts, toasted
- 2 tbsp balsamic vinegar

Instructions:

1. Preheat oven to 375°F (190°C).
2. Toss the beet cubes with olive oil, salt, and pepper.
3. Roast the beets on a baking sheet for 30-40 minutes, until tender.
4. In a large bowl, combine mixed greens, roasted beets, goat cheese, and toasted walnuts.
5. Drizzle with balsamic vinegar before serving.

Classic Clam Chowder
Ingredients:

- 2 tbsp butter
- 1 small onion, diced
- 2 celery stalks, diced
- 2 cloves garlic, minced
- 2 cups potatoes, peeled and diced
- 4 cups clam juice
- 1/2 cup heavy cream
- 1 can (6.5 oz) chopped clams, drained
- Salt and pepper
- Fresh parsley, chopped (for garnish)

Instructions:

1. In a large pot, melt butter over medium heat.
2. Add onion, celery, and garlic. Sauté for 5 minutes, until softened.
3. Add potatoes and clam juice. Bring to a boil, then reduce heat and simmer for 15-20 minutes, until potatoes are tender.
4. Stir in heavy cream and clams. Simmer for an additional 5 minutes.
5. Season with salt and pepper, and garnish with fresh parsley.
6. Serve hot.

Chicken Fried Rice with Vegetables

Ingredients:

- 2 tbsp sesame oil
- 2 boneless, skinless chicken breasts, diced
- 2 eggs, scrambled
- 1/2 cup frozen peas and carrots
- 4 cups cooked rice (preferably day-old)
- 2 tbsp soy sauce
- 1 tbsp oyster sauce
- 2 green onions, chopped
- Salt and pepper

Instructions:

1. Heat sesame oil in a large skillet over medium-high heat.
2. Add chicken and cook for 5-7 minutes, until browned and cooked through.
3. Push the chicken to one side of the skillet. Add eggs to the other side and scramble until cooked.
4. Add peas and carrots, cooking for 3-4 minutes, until heated through.
5. Add the rice, soy sauce, oyster sauce, and green onions. Stir to combine and cook for 5 minutes, until the rice is hot and lightly crispy.
6. Season with salt and pepper to taste.
7. Serve hot.

www.ingramcontent.com/pod-product-compliance
Lightning Source LLC
LaVergne TN
LVHW081318060526
838201LV00055B/2342